LEARN ABOUT DIRT

BY PAMELA HALL

Published by The Child's World®
1980 Lookout Drive • Mankato, MN 56003-1705
800-599-READ • www.childsworld.com

ACKNOWLEDGMENTS
The Child's World®: Mary Berendes, Publishing Director
Content Consultant: Paige Novak, PhD, Associate Professor of Environmental Engineering
University of Minnesota
The Design Lab: Design and production
Red Line Editorial: Editorial direction

PHOTO CREDITS: iStockphoto, cover, 1, 2, 3, 4, 6, 8, 10, 11, 12, 14, 16, 18, 20, 22; ParkerDeen/iStockphoto, 5; 13, 17 (bottom), 19 (bottom), 21; Alexander Raths/Fotolia, 7 (top); Milan Jurkovic/Fotolia, 7 (bottom); Jane Yamada, 9, 23; Claudia Dewald/iStockphoto, 15; Peggy Boegner/Fotolia, 17 (top); Jim Parkin/Fotolia, 19 (top)

LIBRARY OF CONGRESS CATALOGING-IN-PUBLICATION DATA
Hall, Pamela.
Dig in! learn about dirt / by Pamela Hall, Illustrated by Jane Yamada.
p. cm.
ISBN 978-1-60253-507-7 (library bound : alk. paper)
1. Soils—Juvenile literature. I. Yamada, Jane. II. Title.
S591.3.D55 2010
631.4—dc22 2010010974

Printed in the United States of America in Mankato, Minnesota.
July 2010
F11538

CONTENTS

Delightful Dirt

Dig it.

Plant in it.

Lift it.

Sift it through your fingers.

Spongy, sandy, or sticky—
it's all delightful dirt!

Dirt is delightful to play in! ▸

Where Is Dirt?

Soil is another word for dirt.
Soil covers most of Earth's land.
Sometimes, soil is easy to see.

But soil is also under sidewalks and roads. It swirls in lakes and streams. It blows in the wind.

We plant gardens in soil. ▶

Soil at the bottom of a lake looks different from soil in a garden. ▶

Sand, Silt, and Clay

Scoop up some dirt.
Does it feel dry and grainy?
That could be sand.

Does it feel powdery or slippery?
That could be **silt**.

Is it sticky?
That could be **clay**.

Together, sand, silt, and clay make up most of soil.

This is how grains of sand, silt, and clay would look under a microscope. Imagine how tiny a single grain of sand is. Silt and clay grains are even smaller. ▸

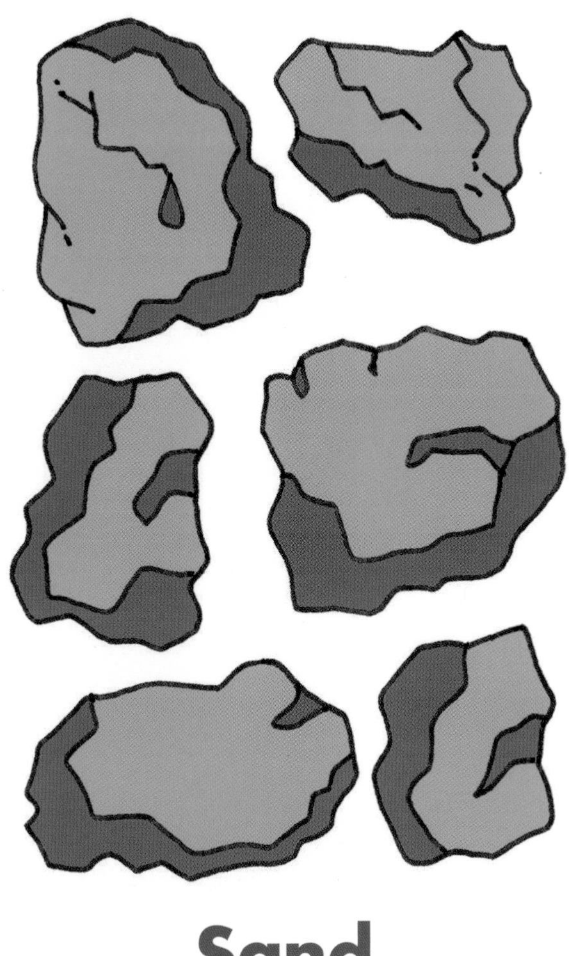

Sand

Silt

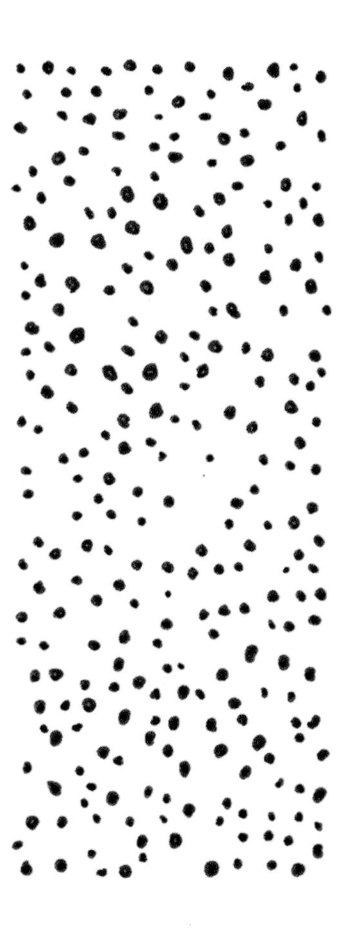

Clay

Sand, silt, and clay were once
part of bigger rocks.
The big rocks wore away.

Rain and wind beat down on them.
Ice cracked them.
The hot sun crumbled them.
Over thousands of years, soil piled up.

Ice, wind, rain, and sun work like sandpaper to wear down even the biggest rocks. ▸

Rich, Black Humus

Is your soil dark and wet?
It could have a good amount of **humus**.
This is the richest part of dirt.
It helps plants grow.

Soil rich in humus has **nutrients** plants need. ▸

Humus began with dead plants and animals.
It also needed millions of tiny creatures.
These creatures live in soil.
Most of them are so small you would need a microscope to see them.

The creatures break down leaves, bones, and more. They turn dead things into rich, dark humus.

In one handful of dirt could be more tiny creatures than all the people on Earth!

Air and Water

Is your soil loose and crumbly?
It has lots of air spaces in it.
Plant roots may have made the soil loose.
Wriggling worms and other animals probably helped, too.

Loose soil lets water drip down.
Plants suck up the water through their roots. Soil's living creatures do best when their home has plenty of air and water.

Moles loosen soil by digging tunnels under the ground. ▶

Roots spread out to help hold plants in place. ▶

Mix It Up

Compare a desert and a farm.
Both are covered in soil.
But the soil in each place is very different.

Soil's ingredients mix in different ways.
Soil is different in different places.

Desert soil is often dry and rocky. ▶

The best farm soil is dark and moist. ▶

Soil can change for many reasons.

These include:

what the weather is like,
the way the land is,
which plants are growing in it,
which creatures live in it,
and how people farm it.

Farmers have to take care of soil to make sure it is good for plants. ▶

We Need Dirt!

But one thing is certain.
You eat plants that grow in soil.
Or you eat animals that eat those plants.
Without soil, there would be no food.
Believe it or not, your life depends on dirt!

What Makes Dirt?

Words to Know

clay (KLAY): Clay is made of the smallest rock pieces in soil. Clay makes sticky soil.

humus (HYOO-muss): Humus is rich, dark soil made from dead plants and animals. Humus makes good soil for a garden.

nutrients (NOO-tree-uhnts): Nutrients are used by living things to stay healthy. Humus has lots of nutrients.

silt (SILT): Silt is made of very small rock pieces in soil. Silt is powdery, like baking flour.

soil (SOY-il): Soil is the word scientists use for dirt. Soil covers most of Earth's land.